An act of
Love

BASIC
BIBLE
TRUTHS
PUBLICATIONS

2212 Bellevue Rd.
Dublin, GA. 31021
basicbibletruth.org

A study guide designed to help one understand not only the need for discipline, but also the manner in which it is to be done.

DEDICATION

For the past thirty-four years there has been one person who has stood by my side and supported me. It is only right this book should be dedicated to her. My loving and forgiving wife Nancy Jean is one of the main reasons I am able to both preach and write as I do. She has been a great encouragement to me at all times. When I wanted to quit and do something else, she helped me with the strength to continue. May God always bless her and give her a long and useful life. When her journey is over, may He give her a home with Him throughout the ages.

ACKNOWLEDGEMENTS

I want to thank two ladies who proof read this book. Nancy Goring and Donna Adcock. Nancy Goring read the first draft and made several comments which helped tremendously with the material. Donna Adcock, secretary for the Wesconnett church of Christ in Jacksonville Florida and a great aid to me with my work, made the finial corrections.

May God always bless us with those who have such great talents.

THE FOREWORD

In my opinion the brotherhood of God's people is blessed beyond measure to have writers within our midst like brother Johnie Scaggs. Not because I suppose he is a "cut above" the rest of us common scribes who often look to put pen to paper, but because he consistently applies the ink to the parchment like few among us. He is forever publishing articles, tracts, pamphlets, and books to grace a brotherhood of readers with the precious truth of God. There is no end to the proliferation of reading material the man produces either as author or editor, and all to the good of God's kingdom. He understands the "power of the pen" and uses his God-given abilities to that end.

I cannot help but note many among our number who have the ability to write just as well and just as often as the author of the booklet you hold in your hand, but they consistently fail to do so. Why? In part, because they quickly discover writing is hard work. It is time consuming, tedious, laborious, and often goes unappreciated by those who need it the most. When just a young preacher, the great Noel Meredith offered me some advice I never forgot: "write some every day," he says. More than anyone else I know brother Scaggs puts this sage counsel into practice. May God continue to bless him with a long life and much opportunity as he persuades us all with the written word "to continue in the grace of God" (Acts 13:43).

In 2 Chronicles 24:16 the text informs us that Jehoiada the priest received his reward כִּי־עָשָׂה טוֹבָה בְּיִשְׂרָאֵל וְעִם הָאֱלֹהִים וּבֵיתוֹ ("because he had done good in Israel, both toward God, and toward his house"). At the end of the way I believe brother Scaggs' eternal reward will be equal to that of this priestly saint who has gone before us.

Stephen Wiggins
March 3, 2010

PREFACE

Once we realize that discipline is an act of love, we will be better equipped to discipline ourselves and those who need to be disciplined.

If you truly love someone, you will want the very best for them and you will act accordingly. My wife and I raised four wonderful children whom we love with all our heart. As we were in the process of raising our children, there were times we needed to discipline them in ways we did not really like. But we understood if we did not discipline them, we would not be showing the kind of love needed.

God's love for us is the same. "And ye have forgotten the exhortation which speaketh unto you as unto children, My son, despise not thou the chastening of the Lord, nor faint when thou art rebuked of him: For whom the Lord loveth he chasteneth, and scourgeth every son whom he receiveth. If ye endure chastening, God dealeth with you as with sons; for what son is he whom the father chasteneth not? But if ye be without chastisement, whereof all are partakers, then are ye bastards, and not sons. Furthermore, we have had fathers of our flesh which corrected us, and we gave them reverence: shall we not much rather be in subjection unto the Father of spirits, and live? For they verily for a few days chastened us after their own pleasure; but he for our profit, that we might be partakers of his holiness. Now no chastening for the present seemeth to be joyous, but grievous: nevertheless afterward it yieldeth the peaceable fruit of righteousness unto them which are exercised thereby" (Heb. 12:5-11).

If God disciplines us because He loves us, then we should be able to see that we likewise must use discipline as an act of love. If we truly love and care about the brethren, we will act in a manner of love toward them.

Feb. 2010

Johnie Scaggs, Jr.

INTRODUCTION

To say there is a great need for an understanding of the doctrine of discipline in the church is an understatement. It has been called the "forgotten command." Perhaps it should be called the neglected command, for most have not forgotten the command; they have just refused to obey it. The motto of many churches today seems to be, "Hear no evil, see no evil – it's not any of our business." Many brethren today neither practice discipline nor teach it from the pulpit or Bible classes. Some would dare teach it but would never practice it. Brethren claim to love the Lord yet, they refuse to obey His command to discipline; however, the Lord said, "If ye love me, keep my commandments" (John 14:15).

The Bible is clear that discipline is needed. Consider these passages:

Moreover, if thy brother shall trespass against thee, go and tell him his fault between thee and him alone: if he shall hear thee, thou hast gained thy brother. But if he will not hear thee, then take with thee one or two more, that in the mouth of two or three witnesses every word may be established. And if he shall neglect to hear them, tell it unto the church: but if he neglect to hear the church, let him be unto thee as an heathen man and a publican (Matt. 18:15-17).

Now I beseech you, brethren, mark them which cause divisions and offences contrary to the doctrine which ye have learned; and avoid them. For they that are such serve not our Lord Jesus Christ, but their own belly; and by good words and fair speeches deceive the hearts of the simple (Rom. 16:17-18).

Now we command you, brethren, in the name of our Lord Jesus Christ, that ye withdraw yourselves from every brother that walketh disorderly, and not after the tradition which he received of us (2 Thess. 3:6).

And if any man obey not our word by this epistle, note that man, and have no company with him, that he may be ashamed. Yet count him not as an enemy, but admonish him as a brother (2 Thess. 3:14-15).

If any man teach otherwise, and consent not to wholesome words, even the words of our Lord Jesus Christ, and to the doctrine which is according to godliness; He is proud, knowing nothing, but doting about questions and strifes of words, whereof cometh envy, strife, railings, evil surmisings, Perverse disputings of men of corrupt minds, and destitute of the truth, supposing that gain is godliness: from such withdraw thyself (1 Tim. 6:3-5).

It is reported commonly that there is fornication among you, and such fornication as is not so much as named among the Gentiles, that one should have his father's wife. And ye are puffed up, and have not rather mourned, that he that hath done this deed might be taken away from among you. For I verily, as absent in body, but present in spirit, have judged already, as though I were present, concerning him that hath so done this deed, In the name of our Lord Jesus Christ, when ye are gathered together, and my spirit, with the power of our Lord Jesus Christ, To deliver such an one unto Satan for the destruction of the flesh, that the spirit may be saved in the day of the Lord Jesus. Your glorying is not good. Know ye not that a little leaven leaveneth the whole lump? Purge out therefore the old leaven, that ye may be a new lump, as ye are unleavened. For even Christ our passover is sacrificed for us: Therefore let us keep the feast, not with old leaven, neither with the leaven of malice and wickedness; but with the unleavened bread of sincerity and truth. I wrote unto you in an epistle not to company with fornicators: Yet not altogether with the fornicators of this world, or with the covetous, or extortioners, or with idolaters; for then must ye needs go out of the world. But now I have written unto you not to keep company, if any man that is called a brother be a fornicator, or covetous, or an idolater, or a railer, or a drunkard, or an extortioner; with such an one no not to eat (1 Cor. 5:1-11).

These verses alone should cause us to understand that discipline is needed in the Lord's body today and if these passages are not heeded, it will be our downfall. Many are uncertain about how to discipline and therefore do not practice it. One preacher stated that one could not show a pattern that is, step by step instructions on how to discipline and therefore, we could not practice it today. However, he fails to understand God does not need to give us a detailed list of how to discipline, but rather the simple command to do so is sufficient.

However, he needs to study his Bible once again and read such passages as Matthew 18:15-20 and 1 Cor. 5:1-ff, for therein we find a pattern for carrying out the command to discipline. Furthermore, the Old Testament has given us many examples of discipline and the "how to" to carry it out (at least in principle) (cf. Joshua 7). These things were written for our learning, "Now all these things happened unto them for ensamples: and they are written for our admonition, upon whom the ends of the world are come" (1 Cor. 10:11). One would think we would not want to make the same mistakes of ancient Israel, but it would seem that perhaps in many places we already have therefore, we need to make correction before it is eternally too late.

On this matter, Ed Smithson said:

> ...we are to judge those that are within (1 Corinthians 5:12) but that God judges them that are without. Jesus said. "He that rejecteth me and receiveth not my saying, hath one that judgeth him: the word that I spake, the same shall judge him in the last day" (John 12:48). The apostle Paul states a principle in Galatians 6:7-8 which says, "for whatsoever a man soweth that shall he also reap. For he that soweth unto his own flesh shall of the flesh reap corruption; but he that soweth unto the spirit shall of the spirit reap eternal life." This principle not only applies to those things which are eternal but also those things in this life. If a man does wrong in his life on earth, he must expect to receive again for the wrong that he has done (Colossians 3:25). 1

One of the reasons the church is not growing today is because we are carrying too much dead weight.

Many churches today are hindered in their work for Christ because disorderly members are unrebuked; because wayward members are not restored; and because careless members are not exhorted and reproved. The results of such failures are numerous; souls are lost, abilities are not used for the Lord, work fails, the purity of the church is defiled, and the church loses its good report in the community. 2

No matter how hard we work, we will not grow until we do something about the excess baggage we carry. This is like the man who decided to borrow a friend's boat and go fishing. He went out in the middle of the night and climbed into the boat, picked up the oars and began to attempt to row the boat to his fishing spot. To his dismay he could not make any progress. Finally, after much labor he gave up and sat down on the bank and waited until daybreak. With the morning light he learned that the boat was chained to a dead log, which he could not see in the darkness. He could not go anywhere, due to the fact that he was trying to drag too much dead weight. The same can be said of many in the church; we are trying to drag too much dead weight. We need to attempt to make the dead weight useful and alive once again or else get rid of it. Numerous are the congregations who have members who need to be disciplined and yet their elders and members set idly by and watch as precious souls are dying and are being eternally lost because their lives are not in harmony with the will of God. A warning: Those who should have said something to those precious souls and did not will one day stand before God on His throne. They will find they are in need of hearing those words, "well done" (Matt. 25:21) but instead will hear, "depart from me" (Matt. 25:41). Remember the word of the Lord as it was given to Ezekiel:

> When I say unto the wicked, Thou shalt surely die; and thou givest him not

warning, nor speakest to warn the wicked from his wicked way, to save his life; the same wicked man shall die in his iniquity; but his blood will I require at thine hand. Yet if thou warn the wicked, and he turn not from his wickedness, nor from his wicked way, he shall die in his iniquity; but thou hast delivered thy soul. Again, When a righteous man doth turn from his righteousness, and commit iniquity, and I lay a stumblingblock before him, he shall die: because thou hast not given him warning, he shall die in his sin, and his righteousness which he hath done shall not be remembered; but his blood will I require at thine hand. Nevertheless if thou warn the righteous man, that the righteous sin not, and he doth not sin, he shall surely live, because he is warned; also thou hast delivered thy soul (Ezek. 3:18-21).

Let us wake up and heed the commandments of God as they relate to church discipline and help our brethren who are lost before they stand before the great I Am.

SIN IN THE CAMP

Whenever there is sin in the camp, the Lord expects us to clean house. That is, He wants us to keep the church pure. "But the wisdom that is from above is first pure, then peaceable, gentle, and easy to be entreated, full of mercy and good fruits, without partiality, and without hypocrisy" (James 3:17). When the Lord returns to take back the church to heaven, it will be pure, "That he might present it to himself a glorious church, not having spot, or wrinkle, or any such thing; but that it should be holy and without blemish" (Eph. 5:27). Keeping the church pure is of the utmost importance. When we became members of the body of Christ, the church, we were purified by our obedience to the truth (cf. Rom. 6:1-17; 1 Pet. 1:2, 18-19). We were washed in the blood of the Lamb (Rev. 7:14). We are to keep ourselves pure (2 Cor. 6:17; 1 Tim. 4:12; 1 Tim. 5:22). God has always wanted His house and His people to be pure.

In the days of Joshua, the Lord had blessed him and the children of Israel because of their devotion to

Him. The Lord commanded them to take the city of Jericho and He gave them detailed instructions of who and what was to be saved and the purpose for such. Rahab the harlot and all she had was to be spared (Joshua 6:22, 25). Furthermore, "But all the silver, and gold, and vessels of brass and iron, are consecrated unto the LORD: they shall come into the treasury of the LORD" (Josh. 6:19), (cf. Josh. 6:24). Everything else was to be destroyed (Josh. 6:17-ff). But not all heeded to the Words of the Lord. We find in the seventh chapter and verse one that the Lord was not happy with the children of Israel. "But the children of Israel committed a trespass in the accursed thing: for Achan, the son of Carmi, the son of Zabdi, the son of Zerah, of the tribe of Judah, took of the accursed thing: and the anger of the LORD was kindled against the children of Israel" (Josh. 7:1). Achan had disobeyed the Lord; he had taken of the accursed thing of Joshua (Josh. 6:18). As Joshua and the children of Israel began to do battle with Ai, they were beaten back. The Lord informed Joshua why, "Israel hath sinned, and they have also transgressed my covenant which I commanded them: for they have even taken of the accursed thing, and have also stolen, and dissembled also, and they have put it even among their own stuff" (Josh. 7:11). The Lord informed Joshua it was time to clean house. He told him that until this deed was taken care of, He would not be with them in their battles against other nations. Hence, by the authority of God, Joshua seeks out the guilty party. Upon finding the one who was guilty, he is taken outside the city and stoned to death according to the Law (Josh. 7:25).

From this event we, as the New Testament church, can learn many lessons; (1) When sin is in the camp, we must get rid of it or the Lord will not bless us as we need to be blessed. As long as sin is in the camp, the church cannot grow, and she will continue to get further away from the Lord. (2) By the sin of one man the whole congregation was deprived of the blessings of God. (3) Sin can exist in the church without the elders and/or members knowing about it. However, we should remember that if one continues in sin, it will eventually be known.

One writer listed these things which we can learn and apply to the church of today.

3. When sin is known to be in the congregation, it is a time for action rather than for prayer. It is true that we are to pray always, and in all things, but it is never true that prayer is a substitute for another command. When God informs an alien sinner to be baptized for the remission of sins, he cannot obtain remission by praying to God. When God instructs the church to withdraw from those who are disorderly, we cannot pray them out, but we must take formal action.

4. The church can only stand against her enemies when she lives up to the profession she makes. Unless the lives of the members preach the same kind of sermon as the tongue of the speaker, the, church will be in disrepute. The prophet Nathan asked David, "Wherefore hast thou despised the commandment of the

Lord, to do evil in his sight?" "... By this deed thou hast given great occasion to the enemies of the Lord to blaspheme" (2 Samuel 12:9, 14).

Paul condemns the Jews for their hypocritical pretence and tells them that they preach a double-standard, one for those who hear and another for themselves, and as a result declares, "For the name of God is blasphemed among the Gentiles through you" (Romans 2: 24). Of sinners in her midst, the church may say as did old Jacob to his murderous sons, "Ye have troubled me to make me stink among the inhabitants of the land" (Genesis 34:30). Often, we are forced to turn our backs unto the enemy when they fling the cruel darts of accusation about the lives of the members. No power on earth can face the church and overthrow it when all of the members are following holiness, without which no man can see the Lord!

5. God's people should not postpone action essential to purifying and cleansing the church. Many times, there are those in the number of disciples who are fearful and fainthearted. They do not want sin condemned publicly in positive terms. They do not want the church to take action about which the world will hear. They would prefer that the world know the church is tolerating sin than to have it learn that the church is made up of those who are living consecrated lives. The Lord said, "You cannot stand before thine enemies, until ye take away the accursed thing" (Joshua 7:13). It is noteworthy that "Joshua rose up early in the morning and brought Israel" (verse 16) and we too should begin at once to cleanse the congregation.

6. The steps leading to sin are outlined in the confession of Achan. "I saw...I coveted . . . took ... hid" (verse 21). If we would not look upon sinful things, we would always be free from sin. However, if we do see them, we should not covet them. "Every man is tempted when he is drawn away of his own lust and enticed. Then lust when it has conceived bringeth forth sin" (James 1:14, 15). Sin produces a guilty conscience, a desire to hide! It is interesting that the first sin followed the very same steps mentioned by Achan. Satan has not changed the bait on his hook from that day to was.

7. The proof of guilt should always be well established before any public discipline is administered. Joshua was not content with the mere acknowledgment of the sin, but sent messengers to the tent, who found the stolen items and brought them to Joshua and all of the children of

Israel and laid them out before the Lord. This would preclude the possibility of any member of Israel later affirming that an innocent man had been punished.

8. The punishment was administered by the entire congregation. It was not the work of Joshua and the elders alone. They guided the body of people in ascertaining the guilty person, the nature of the crime, and the correct penalty. But the discipline was the act of the entire group. "All Israel stoned him with stones" (Joshua 7: 25).

This was in exact conformity with the law. God had stated through Moses, "if there be found among you . . . man or woman, that hath wrought wickedness in the sight of the Lord, thy God. . .. you shall stone them with stones until they die. ... The hands of the witnesses shall be first upon him to put him to death, and afterward the hands of ALL THE PEOPLE. So, thou shalt put the evil away from among you" (Deut. 17:2-7). Incidentally, in this passage is found another statement of the care that should be exercised in determining guilt before action is taken. God said, "If it be told thee, and thou hast heard of it, and enquired diligently and, behold, it be true, and the thing certain." No man can be scripturally disciplined upon mere hearsay. When there is a question, diligent inquiry must be made into the facts of the case, until the truth and certainty of the accusation is established. It was a matter of God's law of justice that no person should be condemned upon the testimony of one man, but two or three witnesses were required to establish an accusation. That principle has been carried into the New Testament.

9. God's wrath is kindled against his people when they knowingly tolerate sin among them. The only way to set aside

that wrath is by getting rid of the sin. The church cannot prosper as long as it places a low estimate upon sin. It must realize that God's people are to be a holy people. There is much in the little word "So" as used in the Bible. After describing in detail the method by which Achan and family received punishment, the record declares, "So the Lord turned from the fierceness of his anger" (verse 26). This means simply that in the manner described was the Lord turned from anger. Let us not forget that the anger of the Lord was directed to the congregation that tolerated the sinner as well as to the guilty person. This is made plain in the first verse of the chapter under consideration.

The question is sometimes asked, "Why did God demand the punishment of the family of Achan as well as the head of the house?" The law established the fact that one who had knowledge of a trespass and refused to make it known, would bear his iniquity (Leviticus 5:1). Those who uphold evil-doers, even of their own kindred, are as guilty as the ones whom they defend, and should be subjected to the same punishment. In the case of Achan all his physical properties and personal possessions were completely covered with the heap of stones, that they might be a witness to the guilt of this man who lost the right to share in the glories of the promised land because of his covetousness.

In the days of Joshua, God dealt with Israel as "children of the flesh" (Romans 9:8), but now he deals with spiritual Israel. If the law that he gave to them was so rigid in its requirements, can we be justified by setting aside or frustrating his spiritual law in these days? Will God recognize a congregation that tolerates within its number those who are covetous, fornicators, idolaters, liars, and otherwise guilty of trespass and transgression? Can we be saved if we emphasize the command which brings people into our fellowship when worthy, and disregard the one by which they should be removed when unworthy? Does God mean it when he commands us in the name of Christ to withdraw ourselves from every brother that walketh disorderly?

If we keep the whole law and yet violate this one point, can we please our Maker? (Clean Church pp.12-16.)

The New Testament reinforces the principle of keeping sin out of the camp. Paul said to the brethren at Corinth,

Be ye not unequally yoked together with unbelievers: for what fellowship hath righteousness with unrighteousness? and what communion hath light with darkness? And what concord hath Christ with Belial? or what part hath he that believeth with an infidel? And what agreement hath the temple of God with idols? for ye are the temple of the living God; as God hath said, I will dwell in them, and walk in them; and I will be their God, and they shall be my people. Wherefore come out from among them, and be ye separate, saith the Lord, and touch not the unclean thing; and I will receive you (2 Cor. 6:14-17).

Even in the New Testament, we are commanded not to touch the unclean thing. The unclean thing of the New Testament would be the same unclean thing of the Old Testament; that is, it is that in which God has forbidden His children to be involved. Some things God has forbidden His children to do and when we do that which is forbidden, then God is angry with us and He will discipline us. When we become involved in the forbidden, we bring those things into the church and cause it to be impure, thus bringing God's wrath upon us. We, as the church, must cleanse the church of all ungodliness.

I grew up on a farm in Southeast Missouri. We learned many very valuable lessons on the farm. One we all know: If you have a bad apple in the bushel of apples, it will rot the remainder of them unless you get it out. This principle is taught in every aspect of life, but many will not apply the same to the "bad apple" in the church. There is no difference! The influence of one bad member in the church will spread throughout the church and cause others to follow their evil influence. For this reason, Paul told Timothy concerning the work of the elders, "For there are many unruly and vain talkers and deceivers, specially they of the circumcision: Whose mouths must be stopped, who subvert whole houses, teaching things which they ought not, for filthy lucre's sake" (Titus 1:10-11). Notice, whose mouths must be stopped. That is those who are unruly and vain talkers and deceivers. In short, the ungodly must be stopped from spreading their influence within the body of Christ.

Remember the words of Paul,

Your glorying is not good. Know ye not that a little leaven leaveneth the whole lump? Purge out therefore the old leaven, that ye may be a new lump, as ye are unleavened. For even Christ our passover is sacrificed for us: Therefore let us keep the feast, not with old leaven, neither with the leaven of malice and wickedness; but with the unleavened bread of sincerity and truth (1 Cor. 5:6-8).

WHAT IS DISCIPLINE?

We cannot deny that the church needs discipline. But just what do we mean when we speak of discipline? Discipline is defined as, "…an admonishing or calling to soundness of mind, or to self-control, is used in 2 Tim. 1:7." 3

> Nelson's Bible Dictionary states;
>
> To train by instruction and control (1 Cor. 9:27). The biblical concept of discipline has both a positive side (instruction, knowledge, and training) and a negative aspect (correction, punishment, and reproof). Those who refuse to submit to God's positive discipline by obeying His laws will experience God's negative discipline through His wrath and judgment. Also see CHASTEN, CHASTISEMENT. 4
>
> C.R. Nichol and R.L. Whiteside stated;
>
> Church discipline pertains to the teaching, training, correction, and development of

its members, having as its end in view their ultimate salvation. One should not entertain the idea that discipline has to do with nothing but getting rid of unruly members. Withdrawal is to be resorted to only when other disciplinary measures fail. 5

Webster stated;

...3 Training which corrects, molds, strengthens, or perfects the mental faculties or moral character. 4 Punishment; 5 a: control gained by enforcing obedience or order b: orderly or prescribed conduct or pattern of behavior; c: self-control. 6 a: rule or system of rules governing conduct or activity. 6

Discipline starts with self. As Paul stated we must learn to bring our own selves under control. "But I keep under my body and bring it into subjection: lest that by any means, when I have preached to others, I myself should be a castaway" (2 Cor. 9:27). It would be difficult for one to help discipline someone else if they have not learned to control their own desires and shortcomings (cf. Matt. 7:1-5).

Paul said,

I beseech you therefore, brethren, by the mercies of God, that ye present your bodies a living sacrifice, holy, acceptable unto God, which is your reasonable service. And be not conformed to this world: but be ye transformed by the renewing of your mind, that ye may prove what is that good, and acceptable, and perfect, will of God (Rom. 12:1,2).

To not be conformed to this world and to be conformed to the Word of God takes discipline. God expects us to also bring ourselves under control.

PREVENTIVE AND CORRECTIVE DISCIPLINE

Discipline is both preventive and corrective. From a preventive view, we need to help members of the body of Christ grow to such a point that corrective discipline is not needed. This will also help them have an understanding that if they do not grow and corrective discipline becomes necessary, it will be carried out according to the law of God.

Robert R. Taylor Jr. stated:

We give ready recognition to the vital importance of prevention in the realms of medicine, safety, education, economy, etc. It is better to prevent an illness than to cure it. It is wiser to prevent an accident than to bandage up the injury. It is far more prudent to prevent our children from getting the wrong education than undo it when once deeply ingrained. It is better to prevent a recession or depression, if possible, than to legislate its cure. The same is true in the realm of religion. There should definitely be preventive measures at work in the church of our Lord. 7

PREVENTIVE DISCIPLINE

To prevent something means to do something about it before it reaches a more serious state. As related to religion, it simple means to help others reach a level of spiritual maturity through teaching and training (discipline) so as to prevent the need of withdrawal of fellowship. Members of the body of Christ need to be disciplined through the means of instruction.

Paul wrote:

All scripture is given by inspiration of God, and is profitable for doctrine, for reproof, for correction, for instruction in righteousness: That the man of God may be perfect, throughly furnished unto all good works (2 Tim. 3:16,17).

Notice: the scriptures are profitable for (1) doctrine, (2) reproof, (3) correction, (4) instruction. Instruction is the idea of teaching or training. This instruction in a perfect world would naturally begin at home; however, we do not live in an ideal world and thus everyone will not be taught the ways of God in the home. Thus, we take people where we find them and begin training them in a preventive manner (Matt. 28:18-20). We instruct them in the doctrine of our Lord so they might be complete, thus reaching a level of spiritual maturity that will enable them to fight the good fight of faith and finish their course, being assured of a home in heaven. Throughout the course of their life as a Christian, it may be needful at times to give some reproof of things which they are doing in order to help them stay on the narrow road that leads to life eternal (Matt. 7:13,14). By reproof we mean as stated by Wuest,

> ...conviction" ... "to rebuke another with
> such effectual wielding of the victorious
> arms of the truth, as to bring him, if not

always to a confession, yet at least to a conviction of his sin (Trench). 7

This will help each to grow as the Lord desires. Many in the church, who have not been disciplined or taught properly, are dull of hearing and do not understand even the first principles of the Word of God. These need to be disciplined in a preventive manner in order that they might grow and become productive in the body of Christ.

The Hebrew writer stated,

Of whom we have many things to say, and hard to be uttered, seeing ye are dull of hearing. For when for the time ye ought to be teachers, ye have need that one teach you again which be the first principles of the oracles of God; and are become such as have need of milk, and not of strong meat. For every one that useth milk is unskilful in the word of righteousness: for he is a babe. But strong meat belongeth to them that are of full age, even those who by reason of use have their senses exercised to discern both good and evil (Heb. 5:11-14).

We should teach babes in Christ how to grow and then do all we can to help them grow. We are quick to baptize the sinner, but we become impatient when we are called upon to help them grow. Jesus said, "Go ye therefore, and teach all nations, baptizing them in the name of the Father, and of the Son, and of the Holy Ghost: Teaching them to observe all things whatsoever I have commanded you: and, lo, I am with you alway, even unto the end of the world. Amen" (Matt. 28:19-20).

Peter wrote,

As newborn babes, desire the sincere milk of the word, that ye may grow thereby" (1 Pet. 2:2). He further stated that one is to grow, "But grow in grace, and in the knowledge of our Lord and Saviour Jesus Christ. To him be glory both now and for ever. Amen (2 Pet. 3:18).

Members of the body of Christ need to be disciplined through the means of exhortations. Paul said, "Preach the word; be instant in season, out of season; reprove, rebuke, exhort with all longsuffering and doctrine" (2 Tim. 4:2). The word "exhort" means to encourage, to help persuade one to take a certain course of action.

Those who come into the church have lived lives that have been totally out of harmony with the will of God. Hence many of them have already developed habits that are very difficult to change (and will not be changed overnight). Because of their previous lifestyle, they will be easy prey for Satan. Some of them will go back into the world due to an improper attitude on their part. However, others will go back into the world because of an improper attitude on our part because we did not show them we truly cared for them and wanted to help them grow in grace of our Lord. I fear that many preachers of the Lord's church today have become so caught up in wanting to be "somebody" in the Lord's body, they have forgotten about those who are babies in Christ and who are struggling with overcoming the ways of the world. We need to understand once again, that our work is to study the Word of God and to teach and exhort those who are lost and dying in a sin-sick world and also to help those who are spiritually weak in our Lord.

When people become discouraged, they will revert back to that which is familiar to them. In the case of babies in Christ, it follows that they will go back into the world. Once this has happened, it becomes even more difficult to gain them back to Christ. The Hebrew writer wrote, "For it is impossible for those who were once enlightened, and have tasted of the heavenly gift, and were made partakers of the Holy Ghost, And have tasted the good word of God, and the powers of the world to come, If they shall fall away, to renew them again unto repentance; seeing they crucify to themselves the Son of God afresh, and put him to an open shame" (Heb. 6:4-6)

Every member of the Lord's body has a responsibility to help the other members keep their lives right with the Lord. The Hebrews writer wrote, "Take heed, brethren, lest there be in any of you an evil heart of unbelief, in departing from the living God. But exhort one another daily, while it is called To day; lest any of you be hardened through the deceitfulness of sin" (Heb. 3:12-13). He also stated, "And let us consider one another to provoke unto love and to good works: Not forsaking the assembling of ourselves together, as the manner of some is; but exhorting one another: and so much the more, as ye see the day approaching" (Heb. 10:24-25). To exhort each other is one of the means which we have to help each other stay in the faith. Through exhortations we can encourage one other to keep pressing toward the high mark of heaven (Phil 3:14).

Barnabas was known as the son of consolation or exhortation. When he came to Antioch, he exhorted the brethren, "Who, when he came, and had seen the grace of God, was glad, and exhorted them all, that with purpose of heart they would cleave unto the Lord" (Acts 11:23).

We should never underestimate the power of exhortations.

CORRECTIVE DISCIPLINE

The corrective side of discipline has to do with things that are to be used when we have exhausted all the avenues of the preventive side of discipline. This is the last resort. When all else fails, we must withdraw from the one who refuses to repent and bring their lives back into oneness with God and the church. Most brethren will stop here; they want to be involved in the preventive discipline, but do not feel that the corrective side of discipline is of any real value. However, they do not understand that one without the other is of no real value.

Robert Taylor wrote;

The Two Kinds Must Be Linked Discipline should be both preventive (instructive) and corrective (punitive) as needed. The latter implies the infliction of punishment. When preventive discipline is practiced with regularity, zeal and without fear or favor corrective or punitive discipline will be needed far less frequently. However, the first will lose much of its impact and effectiveness if the second is never enforced. Christians who truly believe the congregation they attend will practice the full and final steps of corrective discipline, should such become necessary, are much more apt to heed the wise counsel of preventive discipline. The following illustration amply proves this very point. A group of elders were deeply concerned about their high school seniors in the congregation who were facing the problem of what to do relative to the coming Senior Prom. The elders did not want them to attend. They injected real teeth into the request they made. They let it be known that any senior of the congregation who attended would be disfellowshipped with promptness. Not one senior went! These young people and their parents knew their spiritual overseers meant business. This is preventive discipline with the teeth of corrective discipline in the immediate background. More power to elderships with such convictions for the right and pure. May their tribe increase. 9

Our Lord demands that we withdraw ourselves from all those who refuse to live according to His Word. Listen to the words of Paul, "Now we command you, brethren, in the name of our Lord Jesus Christ, that ye withdraw yourselves from every brother that walketh disorderly, and not after the tradition which he received of us" (2 Thess. 3:6). Those who walk disorderly are to be withdrawn from. That is, they are to be marked as men/women who will not obey the commands of the Lord. Paul said, "Perverse disputings of men of corrupt minds, and destitute of the truth, supposing that gain is godliness: from such withdraw thyself" (1 Tim. 6:5). He also wrote, "And if any man obey not our word by this epistle, note that man, and have no company with him, that he may be ashamed" (2 Thess. 3:14).

WHO SHOULD BE DISCIPLINED?

Jesus gave us very clear instructions as to the "how" and "who" is to be disciplined As it relates to a private offense, He stated,

> Moreover if thy brother shall trespass against thee, go and tell him his fault between thee and him alone: if he shall hear thee, thou hast gained thy brother. But if he will not hear thee, then take with thee one or two more, that in the mouth of two or three witnesses every word may be established. And if he shall neglect to hear them, tell it unto the church: but if he neglect to hear the church, let him be unto thee as an heathen man and a publican" (Matt. 18:15-17).

This verse is one of the clearest sections in the Bible as it relates to the topic. Yet, many will read this verse and then forget to apply it to one's life. How many times do we have to remind ourselves and others to re-read this verse and think about how God has directed us in the manner of dealing with problems between two brothers or sisters, etc., in the church? Instead of following God's plan, we often tell everyone else about the problem before dealing with our brother over the matter. That is not in keeping with the context and most certainly is not pleasing to God.

Robert Taylor stated:

In the settlement of private offenses there are four steps: (1) A meeting between the offended and the offender with the offender's taking the lead. (2) If this fails, the offended is to take two or three others in seeking a solution. (3) If this fails, the church is to be informed. (4) If the offender refuses to hear the church, the offender is to be counted as the Gentile and the publican. This amounts to a withdrawal of fellowship. Fellowship is not to be withheld though until compliance has been made with all stated stipulations in this frequently ignored passage. 10

Notice, that if he does not hear the church, verse 17, (the church is the collective body of believers), he is to be looked upon as a "heathen man and a publican." After one has done all that he can to restore the erring and he does not repent, congregational discipline is required; it is not optional!

Furthermore, God stated that when we take such action, He will be there with us; that is, we do these things with His approval or by His authority.

Verily I say unto you, Whatsoever ye shall bind on earth shall be bound in heaven: and whatsoever ye shall loose on earth shall be loosed in heaven. Again I say unto you, That if two of you shall agree on earth as touching any thing that they shall ask, it shall be done for them of my Father which is in heaven. For where two or three are gathered together in my name, there am I in the midst of them (Matt. 18:18-20).

Despite what others may say, I know that when I follow the Lord's instructions, I am on safe ground. Unfortunately, instead of going to their brother with private offenses, some will go tell everyone else about their problem. All this does is cause the problem to escalate. Why can't we just do what God says and go to our brother first? It does work.

The Bible is also very clear about who we should withdraw from when it is not a private matter. We are instructed that we are to discipline: (1) Those who cause division and who sow discord among the brethren. "Now I beseech you, brethren, mark them which cause divisions and offences contrary to the doctrine which ye have learned; and avoid them" (Rom. 16:17). (2) Those who do not teach sound doctrine. "If any man teach otherwise, and consent not to wholesome words, even the words of our Lord Jesus Christ, and to the doctrine which is according to godliness; He is proud, knowing nothing, but doting about questions and strifes of words, whereof cometh envy, strife, railings, evil surmisings, Perverse disputings of men of corrupt minds, and destitute of the truth, supposing that gain is godliness:

from such withdraw thyself" (1 Tim. 6:3-5). (3) Those who are "busybodies" are to be withdrawn from as well (2 Thess. 3:6-14). (4) Those who walk disorderly. "Now we command you, brethren, in the name of our Lord Jesus Christ, that ye withdraw yourselves from every brother that walketh disorderly, and not after the tradition which he received of us" (2 Thess. 3:6).

What does it mean to "walk disorderly?"

A. Adjective. ataktos NT:813 signifies "not keeping order" (a, negative, tasso, "to put in order, arrange"); it was especially a military term, denoting "not keeping rank, insubordinate"; it is used in 1 Thess 5:14, describing certain church members who manifested an insubordinate spirit, whether by excitability or officiousness or idleness. See UNRULY. B. Adverb. ataktos NT:814 signifies "disorderly, with slackness" (like soldiers not keeping rank) 2 Thess 3:6; in v. 11 it is said of those in the church who refused to work and became busybodies (cf. 1 Tim 5:13). C. Verb. atakteo NT:812 signifies "to be out of rank, out of one's place, undisciplined, to behave disorderly": in the military sense, "to break rank"; negatively in 2 Thess 3:7, of the example set by the apostle and his fellow missionaries, in working for their bread while they were at Thessalonica so as not to burden the saints. See BEHAVE. 11

To walk disorderly, therefore, is to walk out of harmony with the teaching of God. It is to disobey those things which the Lord has enjoined us to do. Many sins would fall into this area, such as "forsaking the assembling" of the saints, (Heb. 10:25). It would include those who lie and steal, etc. It would also include those who are immoral in their conduct. Paul addresses this in his letter to the brethren at Corinth (1 Cor. 5:1-5). One of the greatest problems the church faces today is that of immorality. The church is being filled with folks who are living in adultery and their sin remains unquestioned. Many dares not say a word, for fear of losing "members" or of losing their "job." We need to wake up, for the longer we refuse to deal with such matters, the more souls will be lost in eternity.

If we do not deal with sin in the camp, it will soon spread throughout the whole body of believers and then what will we do? The apostle Paul wrote,

> Your glorying is not good. Know ye not that a little leaven leaveneth the whole lump? Purge out therefore the old leaven, that ye may be a new lump, as ye are unleavened. For even Christ our passover is sacrificed for us: Therefore let us keep the feast, not with old leaven, neither with the leaven of malice and wickedness; but with the unleavened bread of sincerity and truth. I wrote unto you in an epistle not to company with fornicators: Yet not altogether with the fornicators of this world, or with the covetous, or extortioners, or with idolaters; for then must ye needs go out of the world. But

now I have written unto you not to keep company, if any man that is called a brother be a fornicator, or covetous, or an idolater, or a railer, or a drunkard, or an extortioner; with such an one no not to eat (1 Cor. 5:6-11).

WHAT IS THE PURPOSE FOR WITHDRAWING FROM THE ERRING CHILD OF GOD?

The Bible is clear on its teaching to the faithful child of God about his responsibility toward the erring child of God. We have the responsibility of helping bring back those who have gone astray. The reason for helping them is to save their soul from eternal damnation, "To deliver such an one unto Satan for the destruction of the flesh, that the spirit may be saved in the day of the Lord Jesus" (1 Cor. 5:5). Paul stated, "Be kindly affectioned one to another with brotherly love; in honour preferring one another" (Rom. 12:10). We should always be ready to help our fellow soldiers. Peter put it this way, "Honour all men. Love the brotherhood. Fear God. Honour the king" (1 Pet. 2:17). Paul tells us what we are to do, "Brethren, if a man be overtaken in a fault, ye which are spiritual, restore such an one in the spirit of meekness; considering thyself, lest thou also be tempted" (Gal. 6:1). James said, Brethren, if any of you do err from the truth, and one convert him; Let him know, that he which converteth the sinner from the error of his way shall save a soul from death, and shall hide a multitude of sins (James 5:19-20).

Robert Taylor stated the purpose of withdrawal in this manner,

> (1) Withdrawal is designed to cause the erring to repent.... (2) Withdrawal is designed to protect the church against the contagious spread of contamination.... (3) Withdrawal is designed to exhibit fully the church's total and unreserved submission to Christ in all things.... (4) Withdrawal should prompt all members to examine themselves and make proper correction of their lives before the ultimate of church discipline faces them."
> 12

Withdrawal of fellowship is thus for the purpose of saving souls from eternal damnation and to help bring one back into fellowship with God. Furthermore, it is designed to help make the church as a whole stronger in the faith.

THE RESPONSIBILITY OF THE CHURCH TOWARD THE WITHDRAWN MEMBER

What role, if any, does the church play in the withdrawal of fellowship from the erring member? The Bible is clear that the church must obey the commands of God on this matter if it is to be effective. When a congregation has elders, they are overseeing the flock (Acts 20:28) and they must take the lead role in withdrawing from the erring and the church must follow (see Heb. 13:17; Titus 1:7-13; 1 Thess. 5:12). All members of the church are to follow the example of their elders in this matter. If the congregation does not have elders, the men of the congregation must take the lead role and the remainder of the congregation must follow their example. Discipline will only work if the entire church is behind the action. Matthew 18:17 shows us that it is the entire church that is involved in the discipline of the member who will not listen to sound words and repent. Paul wrote to the brethren in

Corinth concerning the one who had taken up with his father's wife and stated,

> And ye are puffed up, and have not rather mourned, that he that hath done this deed might be taken away from among you. For I verily, as absent in body, but present in spirit, have judged already, as though I were present, concerning him that hath so done this deed, In the name of our Lord Jesus Christ, when ye are gathered together, and my spirit, with the power of our Lord Jesus Christ, To deliver such an one unto Satan for the destruction of the flesh, that the spirit may be saved in the day of the Lord Jesus (1 Cor. 5:2-5).

Notice he stated, "when ye are gathered together" meaning when the church meets. Let it be known to all that we are not to have fellowship with such a one. In Joshua the 7th chapter the story of Achan is revealed to us. Achan took the accursed thing (verses 11-22). In doing so he sinned against God. Joshua said to him, "Why hast thou troubled us? the LORD shall trouble thee this day. And all Israel stoned him with stones, and burned them with fire, after they had stoned them with stones" (Josh. 7:25). Notice, it was "all Israel" who stoned him. That is, the entire congregation was involved in the act. If we are to be effective in our attempts to restore the erring, we must follow the Lord's pattern. Not only must the entire congregation be as one in this matter; so, must other congregations of the Lord's people. We live in an age where there are many congregations of the Lord's people within driving distance of each other. When another congregation does not honor the decisions of fellow brothers in Christ, it makes it extremely difficult, if not impossible, to restore the erring. When they do not honor decisions of such nature, they become partakers in their evil deeds,

> Whosoever transgresseth, and abideth not in the doctrine of Christ, hath not God. He that abideth in the doctrine of Christ, he hath both the Father and the Son. If there come any unto you, and bring not this doctrine, receive him not into your house,

neither bid him God speed: For he that biddeth him God speed is partaker of his evil deeds (2 John 9-11).

Bill Graddy wrote:

After the New Testament has been taught and followed, if there is no repentance, then the final withdrawal of fellowship must be executed. (Matt. 18:15-17; 1 Cor. 5:1-13; 2 Thess. 3:6.) This should be made known publicly, and this person should be "marked" so that wherever he attends, the congregation will be informed. (Rom. 16:17-19.) If the congregations would follow Romans 16:1-2, then sister congregations would have all the necessary information. Note that we have authority for such; study (Acts 15:23f; 18:27; 1 Cor. 16:10; 2 Cor. 8:23.) If we would practice this doctrine as the Scriptures teach, the disciplinary action would correct him or mark him everywhere as a false teacher. (If a false teacher in one place, why not a false teacher in another place?) (Rom. 16:17-18.) The college, home, individual, and the church must honor the Scriptures, and this includes withdrawing fellowship. (Gal. 3:22.). 13

Those who will not honor these decisions of withdrawal of the disobedient are worthy of discipline themselves and should be marked as ungodly men who do not honor the righteousness of God. Those who refuse to mark them will contribute to their damnation (cf. Ezek. 3:18-21) and as such they will lose their own soul as well.

HOW SHOULD WE TREAT THE ONE THAT IS DISCIPLINED?

The question is often asked, "after one has been withdrawn from, what do we as Christians do in the matter?" That is, "how are we to treat them?" Some would say have nothing to do with them. Some have even gone as far as to teach that we are not to even speak to the one who has been withdrawn from.

Paul says,

> I wrote unto you in an epistle not to company with fornicators: Yet not altogether with the fornicators of this world, or with the covetous, or extortioners, or with idolaters; for then must ye needs go out of the world. But now I have written unto you not to keep company, if any man that is called a brother be a fornicator, or covetous, or an idolater, or a railer, or a drunkard, or an

extortioner; with such an one no not to eat
(1 Cor. 5:9-11).

Notice, Paul says, "with such an one no not to eat." We are forbidden to eat with them.

C.R. Nichol and R. L. Whiteside wrote:

Frequently a withdrawal of fellowship means but little. The guilty party is not made to feel the force of it. Our attitude toward him before and after the withdrawal differs but little, if any. Such a course has a tendency to make the man feel that the church has gone through a meaningless form. Though we have withdrawn from him, he should be "exhorted as a brother;" yet on our social relations with him the Lord tells us that we should "turn away" from him, not to keep company with him, even to the point of refusing to sit down at the table and eat with him. 14

James Pilgrim wrote these words:

Those from whom we retreat are not to be counted as enemies, but as brethren. We are still to admonish them (2 Thess. 3:15). This suggests that we may still have a particular, limited contact with the purged, else how are we to admonish them? Paul defined the relation with them — to admonish them. There are two dangers connected with our contact with such persons. One danger is to completely ignore the person. How can one admonish a fallen brother in this manner? The second danger is to be too friendly, to the point that the brother or sister feels no shame. Let us pray for wisdom that we will not be guilty of destroying the discipline in either of these ways (cf. Jas. 1:5). 15

We are not to have any company with those who have been withdrawn from. Notice what one writer wrote.

> And if any man obey not our word by this epistle, note that man, and have no company with him, that he may be ashamed" (2 Thess. 3:14). Paul told the brethren at Corinth to "...have no company with fornicators..." (1 Cor. 5:9-ff). We are told to "turn away from them" (Rom. 16:17).

In addressing a personal matter that had to come before the church, Jesus taught us that the one who was withdrawn from was to be treated as an "heathen man and a publican" (Matt. 18:17).

It is clear from these passages that we cannot have any company with the disciplined brother or sister. We are not to even eat with them; they are to be treated as a heathen and a publican.

However, the Bible also says, "Yet count him not as an enemy, but admonish him as a brother" (2 Thess. 3:15). By this Paul teaches us that when we see the one who has been disciplined, we are to encourage them to repent, treat them with kindness and plead with them to come back to the Lord in order to save their souls. Let them know you love them and care about their soul and that you pray for them daily.

If we cannot even speak to them or have anything at all to do with them, how can we fulfill the scripture which says, "Brethren, if a man be overtaken in a fault, ye which are spiritual, restore such an one in the spirit of meekness; considering thyself, lest thou also be tempted" (Gal. 6:1)? Remember the words of James, "Brethren, if any of you do err from the truth, and one convert him; Let him know, that he which converteth the sinner from the error of his way shall save a soul from death, and shall hide a multitude of sins" (James 5:19-20).

Bill Jackson wrote this article which is very fitting to this section:

"ADMONISH HIM AS A BROTHER"

In the instruction on withdrawing from a disorderly member of the church, found in 2 Thessalonians 3:6-15, the words are clear: The member has been disorderly (vv. 6, 10-11), and is now to be noted and association with him withheld (v. 14). Paul then adds, "Yet count him not as an enemy, but admonish him as a brother" (v. 15). One asks, "How do you do that?" The first consideration has to do with the basic connection the person has had with you: You have been together in the family of God, as brethren in the Lord! And, for all the sinfulness in his life, he remains your brother and yet still has potential for good and for spirituality if he can be regained. He is not an enemy, except for his manner of life and conduct that is repulsive to the saint. An enemy might be shunned even to the extent that you would never say a word to him, nor he to you. But this is not the case; this is your brother.

So, while you cannot keep company with him, or have meals with him (1 Cor. 5:11) or otherwise deal with him in a fashion wherein he might think you approve of him and his behavior, you can still make contact with him. In what manner? Paul answers, "For purposes of admonishing him." There can be the calls, contacts and even the visits, provided the contact centers on that point. You point out the man's sins to him, express your desire - and God's - that he return to faithfulness, and let that be it! Keep that up as often as you have occasion to speak to him! Thus, AS A BROTHER ONCE FAITHFUL IN THE LORD, and now unfaithful, BUT STILL YOUR BROTHER, you make the brotherly approach to him to urge his restoration to faithfulness. 16

Wayne Price wrote this on this subject:

"No, Not to Eat"

The Apostle Paul wrote the following command to the Corinthian Christians: "But now I have written unto you not to keep company, if any man that is called a brother be a fornicator, or covetous, or an idolater, or a railer, or a drunkard, or an extortioner; with such an one no not to eat" (1 Corinthians 5:11).

Certain questions have been asked: "How absolute is this restriction not to eat?" "Are there any circumstances where a Christian may eat with a sinful brother in Christ?"

Paul had just stated by inspiration (see 1 Cor. 14:37) that a brother guilty of fornication was to be disciplined (5:1). This was to include such an immoral brother being removed from the congregation (v. 2). To the sin of fornication, Paul then adds other vices [such as covetousness (greed), idolatry, reviling (slander), drunkenness and extortion] of which Christians must not be guilty.

He then commands that they are not even to share a common meal with such sinners. How often have you been aware of such folks being disciplined, especially the sin of greed? The truth is that it is often quite difficult to distinguish between one's being a workaholic, and his being a covetous person, isn't it? Furthermore, it seems that these six sins merely represent many more which are not listed.

The point is that the Lord's followers are to be different from the world, different enough so that their everyday lives manifest that they are Christians. The world will always be filled with sinners, and Christians, instead of withdrawing from society, are to be "lights unto the world" (Matt. 5:14). They are sent "into the world" (John 17:18), yet they are not to be "of" the world. John further warns us "Love not the world..." (1 John 2:15-17). Problem? These Corinthians were, by condoning fornication to go undisciplined, permitting the world to come into the church, and bringing reproach upon the church. The very concept of "saint" and "sanctified" are the very opposite of that which they were condoning, even though Paul had addressed them as "saints" earlier (1:2). They were to separate themselves from such sins, and we might add "an such like" (see also Gal. 5:21).

Paul states that Christians are not to mingle with (associate with, keep company with, or be mixed up with) such unfaithful Christians. Notice that Paul (1 Cor. 10:27) and even Christ (Luke 15:1) did not object to eating and drinking with non-Christians. Why treat non-Christians differently than an unfaithful brother in Christ? It appears that in the latter case, Christians might be viewed as endorsing sinful conduct. Since Christians live in a world with non-Christian sinners does not mean they approve of the sinful things the world does, but by condoning sin in the church, it DOES APPEAR that they approve such lifestyles!

What Paul writes is not limited to the sin of fornication. Christians are not to get mixed up with such brethren lest they seem to endorse their sinful life and bring reproach on the church.

Can we associate with them in other ways, such as social activities, invite them to sit with us at the school's ballgames, and have them over to play dominoes, just as long as we don't eat with them? It would appear that this is illustrative of any relationship which would appear to condone unrighteous conduct on the part of an sinful brother. What about inviting that sinful brother to go out with you for a meal so you can visit with him regarding his sinful life? How can a faithful Christian reprove, rebuke, and exhort (1 Tim. 4:2; 3:16) with all longsuffering and doctrine, and never have any contact with such a brother? Hence, it needs to be remembered that TOTAL non-communication is not the right procedure for us to follow, for then how is it possible for us to "admonish him as a brother" (2 Thess. 3:15).

Obviously, if a husband or wife be the individual who is guilty of such a lifestyle, the innocent companion is to still live with that companion. But otherwise, as one has written: "...a conscientious Christian should choose, as far as he can, the company, intercourse (communication), and familiarity of good men, and such as fear God; and avoid, as far as his necessary affairs will permit, the conversation (association) and fellowship of such as St. Paul here describes" (Macknight on the Epistles, p. 157). We dare not get mixed up and mingle with such sinful brethren so that it appears we are approving of their sinful conduct. No social contact that would imply our approval of a brother's sinful conduct is permitted, but that must be tempered by the teaching of 2 Thess. 3:15. 17

The main focus on Paul's statement, is we are not to do anything that would give the brother or sister who has been withdrawn from the idea that we think we are still in fellowship with them as to approve of the manner of life they are now living. We should always have in mind that we want to do all we can to gain them back to the Lord. We must never compromise the truth and do that which God is not pleased with.

OBJECTIONS TO DISCIPLINE

Many have made statements as it relates to discipline that, "you're not showing love," "if you loved the person you would not withdraw from them, etc." However, when we love someone, we care about them so much, we are willing to take strong measures to ensure they do what is right so heaven can be their home. Every time my wife and I disciplined one of our children, we did it because we loved them, and our ultimate goal was to get them to heaven. I remember every spanking my folks gave me, but I do not think they hated me, but I understand they disciplined me because they loved me.

This is exactly how God feels about the matter: For whom the Lord loveth he chasteneth, and scourgeth every son whom he receiveth. If ye endure chastening, God dealeth with you as with sons; for what son is he whom the father chasteneth not? But if ye be without chastisement, whereof all are partakers, then are ye bastards, and not sons. Furthermore we have had fathers of our flesh which corrected us, and we gave them reverence: shall we not much rather be in subjection unto the Father of spirits, and live? For they verily for a few days chastened us after their own pleasure; but he for our profit, that we might be partakers of his holiness. Now no chastening for the present seemeth to be joyous, but grievous: nevertheless afterward it yieldeth the peaceable fruit of righteousness unto them which are exercised thereby (Heb. 12:6-11).

John wrote concerning God's love, "As many as I love, I rebuke and chasten: be zealous therefore, and repent" (Rev. 3:19). What one needs to understand (and this is where the problem is) is that if one should reach the point of needing negative discipline, then that person is in a lost position. If they died in that state, they would lose their eternal soul. What are we to do? Are we to not care for them and let them continue in a state that will lead them to an eternal life with Satan? Or should we obey the command of God and save them from such an existence? I believe the latter is the right thing (yes, the only thing) we can do. Jude said, "And of some have compassion, making a difference: And others save with fear, pulling them out of the fire; hating even the garment spotted by the flesh" (Jude 22,23). James wrote these words, "Let him know, that he which converteth the sinner from the error of his way shall save a soul from death, and shall hide a multitude of sins" (Jam. 5:20).

Some will object and say we have no right to judge others. For this, they attempt to use Matthew 7:1,2, "Judge not, that ye be not judged. For with what judgment ye judge, ye shall be judged: and with what measure ye mete, it shall be measured to you again." They do err not knowing the scriptures. The overall context of Matthew 7 teaches we can, and must, judge others, but we are to make sure when we do judge we are doing so with the blessings of God. Listen to the remainder of what the Lord said,

And why beholdest thou the mote that is in thy brother's eye, but considerest not the beam that is in thine own eye? Or how wilt thou say to thy brother, Let me pull out the mote out of thine eye; and, behold, a beam is in thine own eye? Thou hypocrite, first cast out the beam out of thine own eye; and then shalt thou see clearly to cast out the mote out of thy brother's eye (Matt. 7:3-5).

Later in that same chapter Jesus said,

"Wherefore by their fruits ye shall know them" (Matt. 7:20). Thus, He teaches us once again that we do judge others and in doing so we are not showing a lack of love. It is because of our love for their souls (and our own soul, Ezek. 3:18-21), that we try to help them see the error of their ways and bring them back to the Lord. Some will object and say we are all sinners; therefore, we cannot discipline others. However, they do not understand the scriptures. The Bible nowhere teaches that all of God's children are sinners! It does teach,

If we say that we have no sin, we deceive ourselves, and the truth is not in us. If we confess our sins, he is faithful and just to forgive us our sins, and to cleanse us from all unrighteousness. If we say that we have not sinned, we make him a liar, and his word is not in us (1 John 1:8-10).

To say that we sin is not the same as to say we are all sinners. I, as do all men, sin, but I do not continue to walk in sin. As Paul spoke of those who "walk disorderly" (2 Thess. 3:6), he was referring to those who continued to walk in a disorderly fashion or who continued to live in sin. To say we cannot discipline those who "walk disorderly" because we all have sinned and fallen short of the glory of God is to make passages such as Matthew 7:1-5 and all other passages we have referred to in this lesson worthless. That is, it is without any power or meaning for the child of God today.

Bill Jackson wrote on this matter as such:
We're all sinners" - the point is true, and
the point is not true, some men use it in a
deceitful fashion. Perhaps we can best
see it laid out in this fashion:

Some are sinners because they live a life
of sin, reject all of the efforts made by
God and Christ, spurn all pleadings of the
righteous, and persist in a fleshly lifestyle,
or a sectarian perversion of doctrine, or
both. They're part of that world lying in
wickedness (1 John 5:19). They are in
rebellion to God.

Others, who belong to God through
obedience to his will, and who are now
living for him, would be 'sinners' only in
the sense that they do not live absolutely
perfect lives, as God is perfect. John
points to our sins, and the need to confess
such (1 John 1:8-10). But the child of
God does not live in rebellion, does not
pursue a life of disobedience, and puts

forth great effort to please God. His are the sins of imperfection as he stumbles in always perfectly applying the Standard.

Really, does the Bible speak of Christians as 'sinners'? It speaks of their having sinned, having been lost, having been dead in sin (Eph. 2:1), and then of their having turned from sin, and having, in obedience, received the remission of sins (Acts 2:38) - and it speaks of their need to confess their faults (Matt. 6:12). Never does the Bible speak of the child of God being "a sinner" in the same fashion as the Bible speaks of the disobedient and rebellious man of the flesh being "a sinner." 18

CONCLUSION

To practice discipline is not an easy thing to do. It is very difficult to get elders and members to understand the great need we have today to do all the scriptures teach on this subject as well as others. However, if just one soul is saved through our teaching on this subject, then isn't it worth the effort?

Tommy South wrote,

There are no guarantees that every sinner so confronted will repent. But, contrary to popular belief, some do. It usually takes some time, but people have come back to the Lord, confessing their sins, after being disciplined as Matthew 18 teaches. I have no statistics on this, but even if only one in 100 returns to the Lord, isn't that worth the trouble? Do we really mean what we say about the value of a soul? Practicing discipline will prevent many from being needlessly lost to the kingdom. 19

Let us make sure we obey the Lord, and not man.

ENDNOTES

1. Ed Smithson, "The Forgotten Commandment" (Printed Privately by Ed Smithson, 1965) p. 19.

2. Foster L. Ramsey, "Minister's Monthly – The Discipline of the Church" (Vol. 9, No. 11 – July 1964). p. 538.

3. W.E. Vine, "Expository Dictionary of Old and New Testament Words" (Fleming H. Revell), p. 316.

4. Thomas Nelson, (from Nelson's Illustrated Bible Dictionary, Copyright (c)1986, Thomas Nelson Publishers)

5. C.R. Nichol & R. L. Whiteside, "Sound Doctrine Vol. 3" (Abilene Christian University bookstore) pp. 101-102.

6. Webster, "Webster's New Collegiate Dictionary" (G. & C. Merriam Company, Springfield, MA., 1973) p. 322.

7. Robert R. Taylor, Jr. "The Spiritual Sword" (Getwell Church of Christ, Memphis TN. Vol.5, Number 2, January 1974) p. 36

8. Kenneth S. Wuest, "The Pastoral Epistles in the Greek New Testament" (WM. B. Eerdmans Publishing Co. 1954) pp. 150,151.

9. Robert R. Taylor, Jr. "The Spiritual Sword" (Getwell Church of Christ, Memphis TN. Vol. 5, Number 2, January 1974) pp. 36,37

10. Ibid. p. 37

11. W.E. Vine, "Expository Dictionary of Old and New Testament Words" (Fleming H. Revell), p.320

12. Robert R. Taylor, Jr. "The Spiritual Sword" (Getwell Church of Christ, Memphis TN. Vol. 5, Number 2, January 1974) pp. 38,39.

13 Bill Graddy, "The Church And The Individual Must Honor The Scriptures" (Tract by Bill Graddy) p. 1

14. C.R. Nichol & R.L. Whiteside, "Sound Doctrine, Vol. 3" Reprint by Abilene Christian University). p. 108

15. James Pilgrim, "Withdrawing From The Disorderly" [a tract] (Central Printers & Publishers, 1977). p.10

16. Bill Jackson, "The Southwesterner" June 7, 1989.

17. Wayne Price, "Gems from the Greek, Vol II" (Basic Bible Truths Publications, 2019) p.71

18. Bill Jackson, "The Southwesterner" December 13, 1989.

19. Tommy South, "Gospel Gazette" (2001, Oct.) p. 18.

Made in the USA
Columbia, SC
04 August 2024